THE
PURPOSE
DRIVEN®

Life

WHAT ON EARTH AM I HERE FOR?

by Rick Warren

inspirio

The gift group of Zondervan

RUNNING PRESS
PHILADELPHIA • LONDON

The proprietary trade dress, including the size and format, of this Running Press® Miniature Edition™ is the property of Running Press. It may not be used or reproduced without the express written permission of Running Press.

Library of Congress Control Number 2003100940

Running Press ISBN 0-7624-1684-X
Inspirio ISBN 0-310-80635-6

This book may be ordered by mail from the publisher. Please include $1.00 for postage and handling.
But try your bookstore first!

Running Press Book Publishers
125 South Twenty-second Street
Philadelphia, Pennsylvania 19103-4399

Log onto www.specialfavors.com to order Running Press® Miniature Editions™ with your own custom-made covers!

Visit us on the web!
www.runningpress.com
www.inspiriogifts.com

DEDICATION

This book is dedicated to you. Before you were born, God planned *this moment* in your life. It is no accident that you are holding this book. God *longs* for you to discover the life he created you to live—here on earth, and forever in eternity.

It's in Christ that we find out who we are and what we are living for. Long before we first heard of Christ, . . . he had his eye on us, had designs on us for glorious living, part of the overall purpose he is working out in everything and everyone.

Ephesians 1:11 (Msg)

INTRODUCTION

This is more than a book, it is a guide to a 40-*day spiritual journey* that will enable you to discover the answer to life's most important question: What on earth am I here for? By the end of this journey you will know God's purpose for your life and will understand the big picture—how all the pieces of your life fit together. Having this perspective will reduce your stress, simplify your decisions, increase your satisfaction, and, most important, prepare you for eternity.

YOUR NEXT 40 DAYS

Today the average life span is 25,550 days. That's how long you will live if you are typical. Don't you think it would be a wise use of time to set aside 40 of those days to figure out what God wants you to do with the rest of them?

The Bible is clear that God considers 40 days a spiritually significant time period. Whenever God wanted to prepare someone for his purposes, he took 40 days:

- Noah's life was transformed by 40 days of rain.
- Moses was transformed by 40 days on Mount Sinai.
- The spies were transformed by 40 days in the Promised Land.
- David was transformed by Goliath's 40-day challenge.
- Elijah was transformed when God gave him 40 days of strength from a single meal.
- The entire city of Nineveh was transformed when God gave the people 40 days to change.
- Jesus was empowered by 40 days in the wilderness.

- The disciples were transformed by 40 days with Jesus after his resurrection.

The next 40 days will transform *your* life.

This book is divided into 40 brief chapters. I strongly urge you to *read only one chapter a day*, so you will have time to *think about* the implications for your life. The Bible says, "*Let God transform you into a new person by changing the way you think. Then you will know what God wants you to do*" (Romans 12:2 NLT).

DAY 1

IT ALL STARTS WITH GOD

Verse to Remember:

For everything, absolutely everything, above and below visible and invisible . . . everything got started in him and finds its purpose in him.

Colossians 1:16 (Msg)

It's not about you.

The purpose of your life is far greater than your own personal fulfillment, your peace of mind, or even your happiness. It's far greater than your family, your career, or even your wildest dreams and ambitions. If you want to know why you were placed on this planet, you must begin with God. You were born *by* his purpose and *for* his purpose.

DAY 2

—

YOU ARE NOT AN ACCIDENT

Verse to Remember:

*I am your Creator.
You were in my care
even before you were born.*
Isaiah 44:2a (CEV)

There *is* a God who made you for a reason, and your life has profound meaning! We discover that meaning and purpose *only* when we make God the reference point of our lives. The Message paraphrase of Romans 12:3 says, "*The only accurate way to understand ourselves is by what God is and by what he does for us.*"

This poem by Russell Kelfer sums it up:

You are who you are for a reason.
You're part of an intricate plan.
You're a precious and perfect unique
*   design,*
Called God's special woman or man.
You look like you look for a reason.
Our God made no mistake.
He knit you together within the womb,
You're just what he wanted to make.

The parents you had were the ones
*   he chose,*

And no matter how you may feel,
They were custom-designed with God's
     plan in mind,
And they bear the Master's seal.

No, that trauma you faced was not
     easy.
And God wept that it hurt you so;
But it was allowed to shape your heart
So that into his likeness you'd grow.

You are who you are for a reason,
You've been formed by the Master's
     rod.
You are who you are, beloved,
Because there is a God!

DAY 3

WHAT DRIVES YOUR LIFE?

Verse to Remember:

You, LORD, give perfect peace to those who keep their purpose firm and put their trust in you.
Isaiah 26:3 (TEV)

Without God, life has no purpose, and without purpose, life has no meaning. Without meaning, life has no significance or hope.

We were made to have meaning. This is why people try dubious methods, like astrology or psychics, to discover it. When life has meaning, you can bear almost anything; without it, nothing is bearable.

MADE TO LAST FOREVER

Verse to Remember:

*This world is fading away,
along with everything it craves.
But if you do the will of God,
you will live forever.*

1 John 2:17 (NLT)

Measured against eternity, our time on earth is just a blink of an eye, but the consequences of it will last forever. The deeds of this life are the destiny of the next. We should be *"realizing that every moment we spend in these earthly bodies is time spent away from our eternal home in heaven with Jesus"* (2 Corinthians 5:6 LB). Years ago a popular slogan encouraged people to live each day as "the first day of the rest of your life." Actually, it would be wiser to live each day as if it were the last day of your life.

Matthew Henry said, "It ought to be the business of every day to prepare for our final day."

DAY 5

SEEING LIFE FROM
GOD'S VIEW

Verse to Remember:

*Unless you are faithful in small
matters, you won't be faithful in
large ones.*

Luke 16:10a (NLT)

Life on earth is a Trust. This is a biblical metaphor of life. Our time on earth and our energy, intelligence, opportunities, relationships, and resources are all gifts from God that he has entrusted to our care and management. We are stewards of whatever God gives us. This concept of stewardship begins with the recognition that God is the owner of everything and everyone on earth. The Bible says, "*The world and all that is in it belong to the LORD; the earth and all who live on it are his*" (Psalm 24:1 TEV).

We never really *own* anything during our brief stay on earth. God just *loans* the earth to us while we're here. It was God's property before you arrived, and God will loan it to someone else after you die. You just get to enjoy it for a while.

DAY 6

LIFE IS A TEMPORARY ASSIGNMENT

Verse to Remember:

So we fix our eyes not on what is seen, but on what is unseen. For what is seen is temporary, but what is unseen is eternal.

2 Corinthians 4:18 (NIV)

In God's eyes the greatest heroes of faith are not those who achieve prosperity, success, and power in this life, but those who treat this life as a temporary assignment and serve faithfully, expecting their promised reward in eternity.

Your time on earth is not the complete story of your life. You must wait until heaven for the rest of the chapters. It takes faith to live on earth as a foreigner.

THE REASON FOR EVERYTHING

Verse to Remember:

*Everything comes from
God alone.
Everything lives by his power,
and everything is for his glory.*

Romans 11:36 (LB)

Right now, God is inviting you to live for his glory by fulfilling the purposes he made you for. It's really the only way to live. Everything else is just *existing*. Real life begins by committing yourself completely to Jesus Christ. If you are not sure you have done this, all you need to do is *receive* and *believe*.

First, believe. Believe God loves you and made you for his purposes. Believe you're not an accident. Believe you were made to last forever. Believe God has chosen you to have a relationship with

Jesus, who died on the cross for you. Believe that no matter what you've done, God wants to forgive you.

Second, receive. Receive Jesus into your life as your Lord and Savior. Receive his forgiveness for your sins. Receive his Spirit, who will give you the power to fulfill your life purpose. Wherever you are reading this, I invite you to bow your head and quietly whisper the prayer that will change your eternity: "*Jesus, I believe in you and I receive you.*" Go ahead.

28

DAY 8

PLANNED FOR GOD'S PLEASURE

Verse to Remember:

*The Lord takes pleasure
in his people.*

Psalm 149:4a (TEV)

You were planned for God's pleasure.

The moment you were born into the world, God was there as an unseen witness, *smiling* at your birth. He wanted you alive, and your arrival gave him great pleasure. God did not *need* to create you, but he *chose* to create you for his own enjoyment. You exist for his benefit, his glory, his purpose, and his delight.

Bringing enjoyment to God, living for his pleasure, is the first purpose of your life. When you fully understand this truth, you will never again have a problem with feeling insignificant. It proves your worth. If you are *that* important to God, and he considers you valuable enough to keep with him for eternity, what greater significance could you have? You are a child of God, and you bring pleasure to God like nothing else he has ever created.

DAY 9

WHAT MAKES GOD SMILE?

Verse to Remember:

The Lord is pleased with those who worship him and trust his love.

Psalm 147: 11 (CEV)

You may feel that the only time God is pleased with you is when you're doing "spiritual" activities—like reading the Bible, attending church, praying, or sharing your faith. And you may think God is unconcerned about the other parts of your life. Actually, God enjoys watching *every* detail of your life, whether you are working, playing, resting, or eating. He doesn't miss a single move you make. The Bible tells us, "*The steps of the godly are directed by the LORD. He delights in every detail of their lives*" (Psalm 37:23 NLT).

Every human activity, except sin, can be done for God's pleasure if you do it with an attitude of praise. You can wash dishes, repair a machine, sell a product, write a computer program, grow a crop, and raise a family for the glory of God.

Like a proud parent, God especially enjoys watching you use the talents and abilities he has given you. God intentionally gifted us differently for his enjoyment. He has made some to be athletic and some to be analytical. You may

be gifted at mechanics or mathe-
matics or music or a thousand
other skills. All these abilities can
bring a smile to God's face.

DAY 10

THE HEART OF WORSHIP

Verse to Remember:

Surrender your whole being to him to be used for righteous purposes.

Romans 6:13b (TEV)

Surrendering to God is not passive resignation, fatalism, or an excuse for laziness. It is not accepting the status quo. It may mean the exact opposite: sacrificing your life or suffering in order to change what needs to be changed. God often calls surrendered people to do battle on his behalf. Surrendering is not for cowards or doormats. Likewise, it does not mean giving up rational thinking. God would not waste the mind he gave you! God does not want robots to serve him.

37

Surrendering is not repressing your personality. God wants to use your unique personality. Rather than its being diminished, surrendering enhances it. C. S. Lewis observed, "The more we let God take us over, the more truly ourselves we become—because he made us. He invented all the different people that you and I were intended to be . . . It is when I turn to Christ, when I give up myself to His personality, that I first begin to have a real personality of my own."

DAY 11

BECOMING BEST FRIENDS WITH GOD

Verse to Remember:

*Friendship with God is reserved
for those who reverence him.*

Psalm 25:14a (LB)

You will never grow a close relationship with God by just attending church once a week or even having a daily quiet time. Friendship with God is built by sharing *all* your life experiences with him.

Of course, it is important to establish the habit of a daily devotional time with God, but he wants more than an appointment in your schedule. He wants to be included in *every* activity, *every* conversation, every problem, and even every thought. You can carry on a continuous, open-ended conversation with him throughout your day, talking with him about whatever you are doing or thinking *at that moment.*

DAY 12

─── ❧ ───

DEVELOPING YOUR FRIENDSHIP WITH GOD

Verse to Remember:

Draw close to God, and God will draw close to you.

James 4:8 (NLT)

In the Bible, the friends of God were honest about their feelings, often complaining, second-guessing, accusing, and arguing with their Creator. God, however, didn't seem to be bothered by this frankness; in fact, he encouraged it.

Every time you trust God's wisdom and do whatever he says, even when you don't understand it, you deepen your friendship with God. We don't normally think of obedience as a characteristic of friendship; that's reserved for relationships with a parent or the boss or a superior officer, not a friend. However, Jesus made it clear that obedience is a condition of intimacy with God. He said, "*You are my friends if you do what I command*" (John 15:14 NIV).

The truth is—you are as close to God *as you choose to be*. Intimate friendship with God is a choice, not an accident. You must intentionally seek it. Do you really want it—more than anything? What is it worth to you? Is it worth giving up other things? Is it worth the effort of developing the habits and skills required?

DAY 13

WORSHIP THAT PLEASES GOD

Verse to Remember:

Love the Lord your God with all your heart and with all your soul and with all your mind and with all your strength.

Mark 12:30 (NIV)

God is pleased when our worship is authentic. When Jesus said you must "*worship in spirit*," he wasn't referring to the Holy Spirit, but to *your* spirit. Made in God's image, you are a spirit that resides in a body, and God designed your spirit to communicate with him. Worship is your spirit responding to God's Spirit.

When Jesus said, "*Love God with all your heart and soul*" he meant that worship must be genuine and heartfelt. It is not just a matter of saying the right words;

you must mean what you say.
Heartless praise is not praise at all!
It is worthless, an insult to God.

DAY 14

WHEN GOD SEEMS DISTANT

Verse to Remember:

For God has said, "I will never leave you; I will never abandon you."

Hebrews 13:5 (TEV)

The deepest level of worship is praising God in spite of pain, thanking God during a trial, trusting him when tempted, surrendering while suffering, and loving him when he seems distant.

DAY 15

❧

FORMED FOR GOD'S FAMILY

Verse to Remember:

See how very much our heavenly Father loves us, for he allows us to be called his children, and we really are!

1 John 3:1 (NLT)

50

God wants a family, and he created you to be a part of it. This is God's second purpose for your life, which he planned before you were born. The entire Bible is the story of God building a family who will love him, honor him, and reign with him forever. It says, "*His unchanging plan has always been to adopt us into his own family by bringing us to himself through Jesus Christ. And this gave him great pleasure*" (Ephesians 1:5 NLT).

DAY 16

WHAT MATTERS MOST

Verse to Remember:

*The entire law is summed up
in a single command:
"Love your neighbor as yourself."*
Galatians 5:14 (LB)

Love should be your top priority, primary objective, and greatest ambition. Love is not a *good* part of your life; it's the *most important* part. The Bible says, "*Let love be your greatest aim*" (1 Corinthians 14:1a LB).

It's not enough to say, "*One* of the things I want in life is to be loving," as if it's in your top ten list. Relationships must have priority in your life above everything else. Why? Life without love is really worthless.

DAY 17

A PLACE TO BELONG

Verse to Remember:

In Christ we who are many form one body, and each member belongs to all the others.

Romans 12:5 (NIV)

A church family identifies you as a genuine believer. I can't claim to be following Christ if I'm not committed to any specific group of disciples. Jesus said, "*Your love for one another will prove to the world that you are my disciples*" (John 13:35 NLT).

When we come together in love as a church family from different backgrounds, race, and social status, it is a powerful witness to the world. You are not the Body of Christ on your own. You need others to express that. *Together,* not separated, we are his Body.

❧

EXPERIENCING LIFE TOGETHER

Verse to Remember:

Share each other's troubles and problems, and in this way obey the law of Christ.

Galatians 6:2 (NLT)

God intends for us to experience life together. The Bible calls this shared experience *fellowship*. Today, however, the word has lost most of its biblical meaning. "Fellowship" now usually refers to casual conversation, socializing, food, and fun. The question, "Where do you fellowship?" means "Where do you attend church?" "Stay after for fellowship" usually means "Wait for refreshments."

Real fellowship is so much more than just showing up at services. It is *experiencing life together*. It includes unselfish loving, honest sharing, practical serving, sacrificial giving, sympathetic comforting, and all the other "one another" commands found in the New Testament.

DAY 19

CULTIVATING COMMUNITY

Verse to Remember:

We understand what love is when we realize that Christ gave his life for us. That means we must give our lives for other believers.

1 John 3:16 (GWT)

If you are a member of a small group or class, I urge you to make a group covenant that includes the nine characteristics of biblical fellowship: We will share our true feelings (authenticity), encourage each other (mutuality), support each other (sympathy), forgive each other (mercy), speak the truth in love (honesty), admit our weaknesses (humility), respect our differences, (courtesy), not gossip (confidentiality), and make group a priority (frequency).

When you look at the list of

characteristics, it is obvious why genuine fellowship is so rare. It means giving up our self-centeredness and independence in order to become interdependent. But the benefits of sharing life together far outweigh the costs, and it prepares us for heaven.

DAY 20

RESTORING BROKEN FELLOWSHIP

Verse to Remember:

Do everything possible on your part to live in peace with everybody.

Romans 12:18 (TEV)

With whom do you need to restore fellowship? Don't delay another second. Pause right now and talk to God about that person. Then pick up the phone and begin the process. It takes a lot of effort to restore a relationship. That's why Peter urged, "*Work hard at living in peace with others.*" But when you work for peace, you are doing what God would do. That's why God calls peacemakers his children.

DAY 21

PROTECTING YOUR CHURCH

Verse to Remember:

Let us concentrate on the things which make for harmony and the growth of our fellowship together.

Romans 14:19 (Ph)

Nothing on earth is more valuable to God than his church. He paid the highest price for it, and he wants it protected, especially from the devastating damage that is caused by division, conflict, and disharmony. If you are a part of God's family, it is your responsibility to protect the unity where you fellowship. You are commissioned by Jesus Christ to do everything possible to preserve the unity, protect the fellowship, and promote harmony in your church family and among all believers. The Bible says,

"*Make every effort to keep the unity of the Spirit through the bond of peace*" (Ephesians 4:3 NIV).

DAY 22

CREATED TO BECOME LIKE CHRIST

Verse to Remember:

As the Spirit of the Lord works within us, we become more and more like him and reflect his glory even more.

2 Corinthians 3:18b (NLT)

Becoming like Christ is a long, slow process of growth. Spiritual maturity is neither instant nor automatic; it is a gradual, progressive development that will take the rest of your life. Referring to this process, Paul said, *"This will continue until we are . . . mature, just as Christ is, and we will be completely like him"* (Ephesians 4:13 CEV).

You are a work in progress. Your spiritual transformation in developing the character of Jesus will take the rest of your life, and even then it won't be completed here on earth. It will only be finished when you get to heaven or when Jesus returns. At that point, whatever unfinished work on your character is left will be wrapped up. The Bible says that when we are finally able to see Jesus perfectly, we will become perfectly like him: "*We can't even imagine what we will be like when Christ returns. But we do know that when he comes we will be like him, for we will see him as he really is*" (1 John 3:2 NLT).

DAY 23

HOW WE GROW

Verse to Remember:

*Let God transform you inward-
ly by a complete change of your
mind. Then you will be able to
know the will of God—what is
good and is pleasing to him and
is perfect.*

Romans 12:2b (TEV)

Your heavenly Father's goal is for you to mature and develop the characteristics of Jesus Christ. Sadly, millions of Christians *grow older* but never *grow up*. They are stuck in perpetual spiritual infancy, remaining in diapers and booties. The reason is that they never *intended* to grow.

Spiritual growth is not automatic. It takes an intentional commitment. You must *want* to grow, *decide* to grow, *make an effort* to grow, and *persist* in growing. Discipleship—the process of becoming like Christ—always begins with a decision.

DAY 24

TRANSFORMED BY TRUTH

Verse to Remember:

Jesus said, "If you continue in my word, then are you my disciples indeed; and you shall know the truth, and the truth shall make you free."

John 8:31–32 (KJV)

The Bible is far more than a doctrinal guidebook. God's Word generates life, creates faith, produces change, frightens the Devil, causes miracles, heals hurts, builds character, transforms circumstances, imparts joy, overcomes adversity, defeats temptation, infuses hope, releases power, cleanses our minds, brings things into being, and guarantees our future forever! We cannot live without the Word of God! *Never* take it for granted. You should consider it as essential to your life as food. Job said, "*I have treasured the words of his*

mouth more than my daily bread"
(Job 23:12 NIV).

God's Word is the spiritual nourishment you *must* have to fulfill your purpose. The Bible is called our milk, bread, solid food, and sweet dessert. This four-course meal is the Spirit's menu for spiritual strength and growth. Peter advises us, "*Crave pure spiritual milk, so that by it you may grow up in your salvation*" (1 Peter 2:2 NIV).

DAY 25

※

TRANSFORMED BY TROUBLE

Verse to Remember:

And we know that in all things God works for the good of those who love him, who have been called according to his purpose.

Romans 8:28 (NIV)

God uses problems to draw you closer to himself. The Bible says, "*The Lord is close to the broken-hearted, he rescues those who are crushed in spirit*" (Psalm 34:18 NLT). Your most profound and intimate experiences of worship will likely be in your darkest days—when your heart is broken, when you feel abandoned, when you're out of options, when the pain is great—and you turn to God alone. It is during suffering that we learn to pray our most authentic, heartfelt, honest-to-

God prayers. When we're in pain, we don't have the energy for superficial prayers.

DAY 26

GROWING THROUGH TEMPTATION

Verse to Remember:

God blesses the people who patiently endure testing. Afterward they will receive the crown of life that God has promised to those who love him.

James 1:12 (NLT)

Temptations keep us dependent upon God. Just as the roots grow stronger when wind blows against a tree, so every time you stand up to a temptation you become more like Jesus. When you stumble—which you will—it is not fatal. Instead of giving in or giving up, look up to God, expect him to help you, and remember the reward that is waiting for you: "*When people are tempted and still continue strong, they should be happy. After they have proved their faith, God will reward them with life forever*" (James 1:12 NCV).

DAY 27

DEFEATING TEMPTATION

Verse to Remember:

God is faithful. He will keep the temptation from becoming so strong that you can't stand up against it. When you are tempted, he will show you a way out so that you will not give in to it.

1 Corinthians 10:13b (NLT)

You may sometimes feel that a temptation is too overpowering for you to bear, but that's a lie from Satan. God has promised never to allow more *on* you than he puts *within* you to handle it. He will not permit any temptation that you could not overcome.

DAY 28

IT TAKES TIME

Verse to Remember:

God began doing a good work in you, and I am sure he will continue it until it is finished when Jesus Christ comes again.

Philippians 1:6 (NCV)

Be patient with God and with your-self. One of life's frustrations is that God's timetable is rarely the same as ours. We are often in a hurry when God isn't. You may feel frustrated with the seemingly slow progress you're making in life. Remember that God is never in a hurry but he is always on time. He will use your entire lifetime to prepare you for your role in eternity.

The Bible is filled with examples of how God uses a long process to develop character, especially in leaders. He took eighty years to prepare Moses, including forty in the wilderness. For 14,600 days Moses kept waiting and wondering, "Is it time yet?" But God kept saying, "Not yet."

DAY 29

ACCEPTING YOUR ASSIGNMENT

Verse to Remember:

*For we are God's workmanship,
created in Christ Jesus to do
good works, which God prepared
in advance for us to do.*

Ephesians 2:10 (NIV)

God wants to use you to make a difference in his world. He wants to work through you. What matters is not the *duration* of your life, but the *donation* of it. Not *how long* you lived, but *how* you lived.

If you're not involved in any service or ministry, what excuse have you been using? Abraham was old, Jacob was insecure, Leah was unattractive, Joseph was abused, Moses stuttered, Gideon was poor, Samson was codependent, Rahab was immoral, David had an affair and all kinds of family problems,

Elijah was suicidal, Jeremiah was depressed, Jonah was reluctant, Naomi was a widow, John the Baptist was eccentric to say the least, Peter was impulsive and hot-tempered, Martha worried a lot, the Samaritan woman had several failed marriages, Zacchaeus was unpopular, Thomas had doubts, Paul had poor health, and Timothy was timid. That is quite a variety of misfits, but God used each of them in his service. He will use you, too, if you stop making excuses.

SHAPED FOR SERVING GOD

Verse to Remember:

God works through different men in different ways, but it is the same God who achieves his purposes through them all.

1 Corinthians 12:6 (Ph)

The Bible says, "*We are God's work-manship, created in Christ Jesus to do good works*" (Ephesians 2:10 NIV). Our English word *poem* comes from the Greek word trans-lated "workmanship." You are God's handcrafted work of art. You are not an assembly-line product, mass produced without thought. You are a custom-designed, one-of-a-kind, original masterpiece.

God deliberately shaped and formed you to serve him in a way that makes your ministry unique.

DAY 31

UNDERSTANDING YOUR SHAPE

Verse to Remember:

God has given each of you some special abilities; be sure to use them to help each other, passing on to others God's many kinds of blessings.

1 Peter 4:10 (LB)

Only you can be you.

God designed each of us so there would be no duplication in the world. No one has the exact same mix of factors that make you unique. That means no one else on earth will ever be able to play the role God planned for you. If you don't make your unique contribution to the Body of Christ, it won't be made.

DAY 32

❧

USING WHAT GOD GAVE YOU

Verse to Remember:

*Do your best to present yourself
to God as one approved, a work-
man who does not need to be
ashamed and who correctly han-
dles the word of truth.*

2 Timothy 2:15 (NIV)

Since God knows what's best for you, you should gratefully accept the way he has fashioned you. The Bible says, "*What right have you, a human being, to cross-examine God? The pot has no right to say to the potter: 'Why did you make me this shape?' Surely a potter can do what he likes with the clay!*" (Romans 9:20–21 JB)

Your shape was sovereignly determined by God for *his* purpose, so you shouldn't resent it or reject it. Instead of trying to reshape yourself to be like someone else, you should celebrate the shape God has given only to you. "*Christ has given each of us special abilities— whatever he wants us to have out of his rich storehouse of gifts*" (Ephesians 4:7 LB).

DAY 33

HOW REAL
SERVANTS ACT

Verse to Remember:

*If you give even a cup of cold
water to one of the least of my
followers, you will surely be
rewarded.*

Matthew 10:42 (NLT)

Are you available to God anytime? Can he mess up your plans without you becoming resentful? As a servant, you don't get to pick and choose when or where you will serve. Being a servant means giving up the right to control your schedule and allowing God to interrupt it whenever he needs to.

If you will remind yourself at the start of every day that you are God's servant, interruptions won't frustrate you as much, because your agenda will be whatever God wants to bring into your life. Servants see

interruptions as divine appoint-
ments for ministry and are happy
for the opportunity to practice
serving.

DAY 34

THINKING LIKE A SERVANT

Verse to Remember:

Your attitude should be the same as that of Christ Jesus.

Philippians 2:5 (NIV)

To be a servant requires a mental shift, a change in your attitudes. God is always more interested in *why* we do something than in what we do. Attitudes count more than achievements. King Amaziah lost God's favor because "*he did what was right in the sight of the LORD, yet not with a true heart*" (2 Chronicles 25:2 NRSV).

Servants think more about others than about themselves. Servants focus on others, not themselves. This is true humility: not thinking less of ourselves but thinking of ourselves *less*. They are self-forgetful. Paul said, "*Forget yourselves long enough to lend a helping hand*" (Philippians 2:4 Msg). This is what it means to "lose your life"—forgetting yourself in service to others. When we stop focusing on our own needs, we become aware of the needs around us.

DAY 35:

GOD'S POWER IN YOUR WEAKNESS

Verse to Remember:

*My grace is sufficient for you,
my power is made perfect in
weakness.*

2 Corinthians 12:9a (NIV)

God has never been impressed with strength or self-sufficiency. In fact, he is drawn to people who are weak and admit it. Jesus regarded this recognition of our need as being *"poor in spirit"* (Matthew 5:3). It's the number one attitude he blesses.

The Bible is filled with examples of how God loves to use imperfect, ordinary people to do extraordinary things in spite of their weaknesses. If God only used perfect people, nothing would ever get done, because none of us is flawless. That God uses imperfect people is encouraging news for all of us.

DAY 36

MADE FOR A MISSION

Verse to Remember:

Jesus said, "Go and make disciples of all nations, baptizing them in the name of the Father and of the Son and of the Holy Spirit,

*and teaching them to obey
everything I have commanded
you. And surely I am with you
always, to the very end of the
age."*

Matthew 28:19–20 (NIV)

To fulfill your mission will require that you abandon your agenda and accept God's agenda for your life. You can't just "tack it on" to all the other things you'd like to do with your life. You must say, like Jesus, *"Father, . . . I want your will, not mine"* (Luke 22:42 NLT). You yield your rights, expectations, dreams, plans, and ambitions to him. You stop praying selfish prayers like "God bless what I want to do." Instead you pray, "God help me to do what you're blessing!" You hand God a blank sheet with your name signed at the bottom and tell him to fill in the details. The Bible says, *"Give yourselves completely to God—every part of you . . . to be tools in the hands of God, to be used for his good purposes"* (Romans 6:13b LB).

If you will commit to fulfilling your mission in life no matter what it costs, you will experience the blessing of God in ways that few people ever experience. There is almost nothing God won't do for the man or woman who is committed to serving the kingdom of God.

Jesus has promised, "*[God] will give you all you need from day to day if you live for him and make the Kingdom of God your primary concern*" (Matthew 6:33 NLT).

DAY 37

SβG

SHARING YOUR LIFE MESSAGE

Verse to Remember:

Be ready at all times to answer anyone who asks you to explain the hope you have in you, but do it with gentleness and respect.

1 Peter 3:15b–16 (TEV)

God has given you a Life Message to share. When you became a believer, you also became God's messenger. God wants to speak to the world through you. Paul said, "*We speak the truth before God, as messengers of God*" (2 Corinthians 2:17b NCV).

You may feel you don't have anything to share, but that's the Devil trying to keep you silent. You have a storehouse of experiences that God wants to use to bring others into his family. The Bible says, "*Those who believe in the Son of God have the testimony of God in them*" (1 John 5:10a GWT). Your Life Message has four parts to it:

Your *testimony*: the story of how you began a relationship with Jesus.

Your *life lessons*: the most important lessons God has taught you.

Your *godly passions*: the issues God shaped you to care about most.

The *Good News*: the message of salvation.

DAY 38

BECOMING A WORLD-CLASS CHRISTIAN

Verse to Remember:

Send us around the world with the news of your saving power and your eternal plan for all mankind.

Psalm 67:2 (LB)

To think like a World-Class Christian, shift from self-centered thinking to other-centered thinking. The Bible says, *"My friends, stop thinking like children. Think like mature people"* (1 Corinthians 14:20 CEV). This is the first step to becoming a World-Class Christian. Children only think of themselves, grown-ups think of others. God commands, *"Don't think only about your own affairs but be interested in others, too"* (Philippians 2:4 NLT).

Of course, this is a difficult mental shift because we're naturally self-absorbed and almost all advertising encourages us to think of ourselves. The only way we can make this paradigm switch is by a moment-by-moment dependence on God. Fortunately he doesn't leave us to struggle on our own. *"God has given us his Spirit. That's why we don't think the same way that the people of this world think"* (1 Corinthians 2:12 CEV).

Begin asking the Holy Spirit to help you to think of the spiritual need of unbelievers whenever you talk to them. With practice you can develop the habit of praying silent "breath prayers" for those you encounter. Say, "Father, help me to understand what is keeping this person from knowing you."

BALANCING YOUR LIFE

Verse to Remember:

Live life with a due sense of responsibility, not as those who do not know the meaning of life but as those who do.

Ephesians 5:15 (Ph)

Pass on what you know to others. If you want to keep growing, the best way to learn more is to pass on what you have already learned. Proverbs tells us, "*The one who blesses others is abundantly blessed; those who help others are helped*" (11:25 Msg). Those who pass along insights get more from God.

Now that you understand the purpose of life, it is your responsibility to carry the message to others. God is calling you to be his messenger. Paul said, "*Now I want you to tell these same things to followers who can be trusted to tell others*" (2 Timothy 2:2b CEV). In this book I have passed on to you what others taught me about the purpose of life, now it's your duty to pass that on to others.

DAY 40

LIVING WITH PURPOSE

For David . . . served the purpose of God in his own generation.

Acts 13:36 (NASB)

Paul lived a purpose-driven life. He said, "*I run straight to the goal with purpose in every step*" (1 Corinthians 9:26 NLT). His only reason for living was to fulfill the purposes God had for him. He said, "*For to me, to live is Christ and to die is gain*" (Philippians 1:21 NIV). Paul was not afraid of either living or dying. Either way, he would fulfill God's purposes. He couldn't lose!

One day history will come to a close, but eternity will go on forever. William Carey said, "The future is as bright as the promises of God." When fulfilling your purposes seems tough, don't give in to discouragement. Remember your reward, which will last forever. The Bible says, *"For our light and momentary troubles are achieving for us an eternal glory that far outweighs them all"* (2 Corinthians 4:17 NIV).

Imagine what it is going to be like one day, with all of us standing before the throne of God presenting our lives in deep gratitude and praise to Christ. Together we will say, "*Worthy, Oh Master! Yes, our God! Take the glory! the honor! the power! You created it all; It was created because you wanted it!*" (Revelation 4:11 Msg) We will praise him for his plan and live for his purposes forever!

SOURCES

Text compiled from *The Purpose-Driven® Life* by Rick Warren, Copyright 2002, Zondervan: Grand Rapids, MI.

Scripture marked CEV is taken from the *Contemporary English Version*. Copyright © 1995 by the American Bible Society, New York, NY. Used by permission.

Scripture marked GWT is taken from *God's Word Translation*. Copyright © 1995 by World Publishing, Inc., Grand Rapids, MI. Used by Permission.

Scripture marked JB is from *The New*

Jerusalem Bible. Copyright © Doubleday & Company, Inc., 1985, New York. Used by permission.

the *New Revised Standard Version*, Copyright © 1990 by Zondervan, Grand Rapids, MI. Used by Permission.

Scripture marked Ph is taken from the *New Testament in Modern English* by J. B. Phillips, Copyright © 1958 by Macmillan, New York, NY. Used by Permission.

Scripture marked TEV is taken from the *Good News Bible in Today's English Version*—Second Edition, Copyright © 1992 by American Bible Society. Used by Permission.

This book has been bound using handcraft methods and Smyth-sewn to ensure durability.

Cover illustration © 2002
by Michael Halbert.

The dust jacket was designed
by Matt Goodman.

The interior was designed
by Jan Greenberg.

The text was edited by Pamela Liflander.

The text was set in Galliard and Cancione.